C000170442

Love through a Broken Mirror

Love through a Broken Mirror

an anthology of poems

Dark Dove

PARTRIDGE

To order additional copies of this book, contact
Partridge India
000 800 10062 62
orders.india@partridgepublishing.com

www.partridgepublishing.com/india

Contents

To Madhumita, who, over the years,
has remained as a pillar of strength,
inspiration, courage and love

Peace

I want to be with you ... always..

Where I can empty my mind,

Make my heart bleed

And allow tears to flow freely.

There is no place like that

A perfect paradise.

If I have loved you

You have loved me more

It was never a fair exchange,

My hesitant steps took me far,

At times gripped by fear

And at times filled with joy.

But it took a while to love you completely,

Selfish and vulnerable that I am,

You have loved the insatiable timid lover,

Peace...

My Last Wish...

My last wish is to die awake,

Feeling and seeing the throb

Of the universe coursing through me

Seeing myself in myself,

Possibly for the last time,

I would not want to see

The vanishing world,

Growing fainter by the moment,

But want to feel the moment,

Pregnant with the final possibility

For cessation of desires,

And of facing reality,

Without fear or greed.

Of that love that keeps me awake

Love that is suspended,

But redirected by compassion,

Asking nothing: hating nothing, Doing nothing.

Possibly for the one last time,

I would like to enjoy the

Fleeting experience of life and death

In the slowest animated form,

Which I failed to experience before,

On a distant occasion — many summers away,

Which was another opportunity to Feel the same,

The transition — when I was born.

But I didn't see or feel that classic moment,

Or I have forgotten it,

Only the shock waves still resonate in

My now frail body — a body that has no further use,

I failed to feel that moment of birth,

Where my life in my mother womb died

A joyful death — mistaken as a trauma

Making me cry.

This time it would be different,

I would not cry, nor beg for more,

Nor turn my back to this moment in fright,

Instead, I would like to smile

A smile tinged with the kindness of love,

Love, which neither accepts nor rejects,

I wish to die awake.

For Whom?

Flowers in the park — in neat rows,

For whom do they bloom?

To satisfy the sense of order and beauty,

Conjured by an insecure thinking mind.

Why should they ever care?

For order or for disorder,

For sanity or for beauty,

Or for what I imagine or anticipate,

They just live,

Live beautifully — wild and bold.

A grand moment in timeless space,

With the touch of the moist earth,

Warmth of the sun on their coloured cheeks,

Witnessing the perpetual dance of bees,

Or finding a place in the oiled tresses of a woman,

Without a care for certainty,

About their own coming, being, becoming or vanishing,

They just live and die.

Spreading their fragrance in the spring air,

Or releasing the stench in the garbage heap.

The City Choir

Every urban sound is a sound of disconnect,

Of pain, suffering and separation,

Of intense struggle for survival — pain

The only way we know,

That wounds a mother's heart.

The city loves us like a jealous cat,

Never allowing us out of her sight,

Watching over its kittens,

Oblivious of death that stalks every moment,

Where every wall, casts its long shadows,

Closing on us with its assured cold touch,

Of miracles yet to happen —

Of ivory dreams, of gold, glitter and fame,

Of wine and women and flirtatious looks,

In guise of love and pain,

That makes stories and poems,

Sunlight tries its best to penetrate,

The dense thick fabric of living pain,

Trying to lighten the burden of despair,

To touch throbbing heart beats,

But in vain.

Who cares?

No time to stop and look above.

The silver of moon is no consolation either,

Too faint to trace a line,

In the intense rhythmic noise of things,

But in between the mayhem,

Few cracks still appear unannounced,

That take wings,

To fly anywhere, to run away from the din,

To bask in the green

Or to touch the blue with frail fingers,

Withered by the incessant fight,

The lonely crow sits grimly,

On the high iron gate,

Deciding the next wiser move,

But stays glued to its anchor,

Immobile, listening haplessly,

The cacophony of auto-rickshaws,

Revving the bleeding heart of the city,

In the dead heat of night,

Asking for blood, sweat and toil.

Unending is the sad story.

Shadows of Life

Shadows of the ancient Chatim tree,

Sweeps the lawn all day long;

Grass smiles, insects buzz, birds peck,

Enjoying the coolness of the shade;

Life as a fairy ballerina gently floats by.

But the pious shadow seen only in light,

Continues to breathe in the dark —

A persistent oil smudge,

Rewriting the letters of destiny,

Suckling them back to life,

Only a whisper is enough.

Bliss

Remembering our first walk

To edge of the shore,

Shy, blushing, coyly alive,

Love radiating in circles,

From where we stood,

Piercing the sacrosanct horizon,

Where blue meets blue.

The footprints of our tender hearts,

On the wet sand, shaped by time,

Recording our story of togetherness,

With the ebullient waves as witness,

Who waited just long enough,

Before mingling into far away space —

Unsayable and Unknowable,

Our common ancestor.

As water played with us,

Courage soothingly shored up,

Igniting unfamiliar newness,

In the misty evening air,

Honeyed alive.

Just then the wind spoke,

Splaying strands of your long hair,

Across my enlivened face,

And the shameless moon,

Out of her curiosity,

Suddenly dashed across the darkening sky,

Inviting us with her silky light,

Our first salt laden earthy kiss,

Suspended dazzled bliss!

When You Left Me Alone

When you left me alone,

In your going home,

You became a shiver of joy,

A quiet sound of merriment,

A passing flash of light,

In a haze filled empty sky.

When the flight took off,

You never reappeared,

You became an angel,

Drinking the nectar of void.

When I left you at the gate,

You were half leaving; half staying,

Half there; half gone,

When I went home,

It was like coming back ashore,

Where I could get the lingering fragrant taste,

Touched by impatient waves,

Left behind by in your wake,

To sense you in unfettered flight,

Drawn to my own void,

From where I came,

And to find you there,

And not here in the flow of things,

And not here in the things I kept,

Carefully built and stored for you.

I love you,

In the turn, twist and flow

Around the unmoving, unbridled centre of all flowing
moments,

Washed upon my shore

By the ebb and tide of time.

As you fade,

My mind aches in your fleeting wake,

Remembering moments like an impermanent moon,

Growing from wax to wane,

Slowing turning on clarity with care,

Right from the start, long feared,

Long lost, long fought memories of pain and love,

Nothing disappeared.

You would not fade in me,

You would come back home,

To keep it ready

The only place I really like to be,

I have nowhere to go,

But to come home,

Drawn by the tides of

Sudden appearances and disappearances.

As you leave me,

I find nothing in my hands,

But a magic pencil,

Free to sketch stories by itself,

Unaided and unguided by my mind,

Nothing in my ears,

Save the sound of unknown feeble voice,

Whispering the immortal

Rhythm of appearances and disappearances,

Punctuated by silence,

Filled in between by violence and love.

Now from the ground,

I see your loving hands,

Lift me up to the bosom of time,

Sensing your warm face against mine,

Calling me in familiar voice,

Fulfilling my destiny,

Singing me lullabies —

All ancient and future one,

For us to live by,

Whenever, I am back home with you.

Live again

Harsh Indian summer,

Baby green leaves,

Birds chirping merrily,

Pigeons chase each other,

In merry abandon,

Over lowly dew laced grass,

Bracing to meet the sun,

A perfect picture.

I hear the wind rustle playfully,

Scattering the paper on my table,

Papers which carry imprints

Of my dark worries,

Imagined fears of the past,

Fears of an uncertain future,

And of insatiable greed,

Unbridled ego of trying to be something

My body stiffens with unexplained aches.

A sudden draft brings with it,

The smell of sweet flowers from,

Unkempt bushes and shrubs,

Urging me to live again,

Without trying to be anything else,

Just being myself.

My First Love

These hot listless April nights of Kolkata

Remind me of one such night in Farakka,

The night was more alive with brighter and cleaner stars,

The darkness of that night was perfumed with faint gusts,

From the blossoming trees and shrubs,

Carrying with it the earthy wetness of the Ganges bank,

And the invisible greenness of paddy fields that lay beyond.

There was silence,

But a silence that breathed,

The soft undulated breathing of the Ganges,

That meandered along

As if guided by the insistent bass croaking of frogs and crickets,

Incessantly praying for rains or for the stars to appear,

Emerged a picture of immaculate perfection.

Far away from my living quarters,

The passage of Gaur Express,

Was like a long caress, moving with inexorable gentleness,

Across the warm living body of a palpable night.

Suddenly the unseen strain of a Bhatiali song of a fisherman,

Began to trace new patterns on the star lit night.

And that is when I made my first love.

Love the Silence

Time has come with the sunset clouds,

When with joy I greet the stranger

In myself, in my home and at my desk,

Where I labour tapping keys on my laptop,

We look into each other,

Finding each other as long-lost soulmates,

A mate, whom I was ashamed of.

Hidden from public view,

But the persistent stranger,

Loved me much more than I did,

Followed me every moment

Witnessing all that I did,

Never judging me.

Just seeing, an eternal witness,

Now I see more clearly,

The strange mate within me — a unknown friend.

Of whom I was so ashamed; so unaware of.

Time has come to let go of that shame and the hatred,
Time to let go of that greedy attachment to my
imagined self

The dream image of myself,
The dream pasted on my ambitions,
And in my countless conversations,
In my ego; in my arrogance,
And on the internet.
Time to take off that grand dream of being what I
am not,
So carefully constructed in emptiness – meaningless,
And love the strange silent fellow within,
No, just being him,
Because I am simply him,
Boundless is the joy - never imagined.

Summer of 2016

White heat;

A drunk river.

A ferry ghat;

Scorched wooden logs.

Shadows of limp trees;

On drowsy grass.

Drooping eyes of my dog;

Parched throats of birds.

Stooped old man;

Trudging his way to market.

Moments noticed;

Moments unnoticed.

Steeped in reflection;

Of a failed monsoon.

How?

How did all this happen? You ask.

Then visit the rickety serpentine lanes

Of Raja Lane or Tamer Lane of North Kolkata

Where sun fails to reach

Where everything is so bound

By rusty wires of ironclad traditions

Where parents bled their wrists in the bubbling rivers
of their sons

Then you may possibly sense it.

Or follow the path of dark airy rooms of elite institutions

Where death stalks every child every moment

Or follow the dreams of a child,

Laden with the adventurous risks of youth.

Or read the Buddhist texts, the Bible or the Koran

Or read the Ramayana or the Mahabharata

Or follow the struggles of an ordinary emotional man,

Entwined in the loving embrace of his lover

Both trying to walk paths that even didn't exist

Bleeding their way through thickets, swamps, open lands,

At times, resting in inviting valleys and cool green shades.

Or follow the sun kissed ridges both lofty and small

And then you may possibly understand how.

I Can Never Say Goodbye

I can never forget or say goodbye,

To anyone or anything

I like, or don't like or neither like or don't like,

I can never say goodbye,

To anyone or anything,

Even if loved, unloved, uncared or ignored,

Since it is the same me that clings,

To numerous small and big events and egos.

I can never say goodbye,

To anyone or anything, even if —

New cycles begin or close,

Since it is the same wave that changes shape with time,

Over and over again,

Without the ocean that it comes from,

Changing shape or character.

Opinions and judgements don't matter anymore,

Since these are churned from the fleeting dews swept
by winds of that ocean,
Twisting, scaling and shifting moment to moment,
One for each, which others can't see or read,
Hence, I can never say goodbye to —
Anyone or anything.

With You

With you I never feel cold,

Even under a wintry starlit sky.

Walking in dark silent woods,

Bathed by an anemic full moon.

Whose silence is decorated

By beating of synchronized hearts,

Interrupted by a screeching owl

And by your timid steps -

Caressing reality in trepidation,

Seeking assurance.

With you I never feel cold,

Your warmth fills me,

Without overloads of ephemeral cravings.

But between two of us,

Rippling sensations rustle through

Like the calm haste of leaves in spring,

Blown by the gentle river wind,

Carrying a fragrance stronger

Than the most beautiful rose,

Doubled by the love filled embrace of animated trees.

With you I never feel cold,

Touched by the burning moon,

We know how much we love each other,

Like a sweet flower -

Whom one can't but love.

Seeing and exchanging in silence

Coy glances, warm touches, unspoken words.

Walking in step in the woods,

Without the veil of fear in between.

Electrifying!

You are indescribable

There is no doubt that you are beautiful,

There is no doubt about that.

With you I am peaceful,

Without a care in the world,

All worries thrown to the winds.

In your presence, I forget myself,

With no sense of being within or without,

It is love all through,

Inseparable and flowing.

But when I want to describe you,

Words come back – frightened,

Trembling from uncertainty,

Devoid of energy or life of their own.

Words confuse and contradict what I want to say.

Your beauty and joy are truly indescribable,

Let it be so; I could care less,

You live in my heart; and so be it.

It is love, love and love alone.

This morning

This morning is a sad morning

Not that the sun is in a haze

Or the grass is not alive with freshness

Or that the birds have stopped singing.

Still this morning is sad,

There are many things to be sad about.

Like my parents I loved so dearly,

Can't be reached or touched.

Or my shoulders and back pain so much

With the dull pain of feelings - hurt.

Or the sons I loved and clung to

Have long flown the nest urged by their own mental chatter.

Or the dog who never failed to cuddle up in bed,

Left behind only photos to weep silently.

Or my love to paint — warm, dull or morbid,

Doesn't stir in me the faintest will to doodle.

Or the love of my grandparents — their warm touch,

Lost when they left their bodies.

Or the fact that I loved you every moment

And sometimes you cared to sync to my madness.

I remember the honey coloured nights, the close embraces,

With your long hair softly sweeping my bare shoulders.

Everything that I held dear,

Are slipping, going but never yet gone.

Still I search for love — to love in some ways and be loved too,

Though I know that it would always end — leaving pain in its wake.

The unending pain of the softest memories and fondest greed,

More painful, since remembering is timeless though an empty skin.

Awaiting Death

I would prefer patiently awaiting death;

Than patiently preparing for death that awaits.

It is better to know that it can happen any moment,

Than trying to imagine when and how that might be.

In any case I would still remain the same,

Noticing every moment as it happens;

The beginning, middle and the end.

When everything is known & no more questions to ask;

When there is nothing more to love or hate;

When there is nothing more to like and aspire for;

When everything is done;

And nothing more to desire: no answers to seek;

It is better to await death as a desire,

Than prepare for any desirable death.

When there is nothing much to talk about;

When all experiences come to naught;

When there is nothing more one can pass on;

When life is still, meaningless and empty;

When there is no longer any yearning for peace:

It is better to await death peacefully;

Than prepare for a peaceful death.

When there is nothing more to fear;

When the amygdala does not disturb anymore;

When everything can be witnessed clearly;

When underlying meaninglessness is seen in everything;

And emptiness stares in the face:

It is better to await death with calmness;

Than prepare for a calm death.

When everything was loved from the bottom of the
heart;

And there is nothing more to love;

And no more intensity can be injected.

When love is returned in every possible way -
Misunderstood, rejected, forlorn:

It is better to await death with love,

Than prepare for a lovely death.

When all games are played and seen;

When no more games need be invented;

When there is nothing more to expect;

Nothing more to be envious about;

Realizing that there is nothing perfect:

It is better to await death in all its perfection,

Than prepare for a perfect death.

When nothing stirs the mind anymore;

When no problem seems like one;

When puzzles puzzle no more;

And all problems are solved in a stroke;

When senses have not forsaken:

It is better to await death mindfully,

Than prepare for a mindless death.

When there is nothing much to be noticed;

When there is nothing much to be engaged with;

When there is nothing much to be thought over;

When there is nothing much to be exchanged;

When there is no further surprises left waiting:

It is better to await death, unnoticed.

Than prepared for a noticeable death.

Love Fear Trust

My emotions are coloured by fear.

Some relationships are built on trust.

Would fear and trust be strange bedfellows?

Where fear lies; trust belies,

Where trust dominates; emotion flies,

What transcends fear?

What lures trust?

What helps us live in trust without fear?

Is it beyond my intellect?

Or is it compassion, if you will.

Seeing myself in everything,

The same thing over and over again.

Or is it love which does not expect?

Love which allows freedom and space,

Love which is selfless,

Love which allows to grow and live our ways,

Love which has seen both death and life,

In every breath.

Love is knowledge beyond my thinking mind,

It is the attention behind my mind,

Shaping intents; powering movements,

The giver sharing what I have,

The speaker speaking my soul,

The feeler; the knower; the seer.

Touching the end of the Universe,

Only to go beyond,

In every breath.

Flowing rhythmic and chaotic waves,

Letting its light shine through every atom of existence,

Like the invisible salt in our food,

Or like the invisible lemon in the lemon juice

Or like the raindrops in the book

Or like the invisible breath of freedom.

The universe folds in me as I unfold into the Universe.

Unbounded by my skin, bones and a thinking mind,

Bliss — untouched, pure and serene!

A Sad Life

There is nothing more real, more obvious,

More tangible than pain and sadness,

Where we can flow unchained in suffering,

Where all our senses can play

Allowing us to see the obvious,

Feel our pretensions,

And our unbridled passions and false images,

We build around ourselves; for ourselves,

Yet we choose not to see it completely,

Or we choose to ignore it at times.

Absorbed in other worlds created by our unabashed minds,

Silently suffer pain & nurse invisible scars.

Of trying to be what we are not,

Trying to control everyone and everything else

Save ourselves.

Failing, wailing, crying,

But the world does not change the way we want,

Making us sad.

Yet I choose not to change not myself,

Or see not the false images,

Or not listen to false voices within,

Feel not: See not; Trust not,

But rush through mindlessly.

The dark maze

Of not seeing the obvious,

Of not engaging with the what I see,

Of not making the crazy choices

Of not expressing what my soul deeply wants.

So timid; so afraid; so personality filled,

All the sadness of life lies in that vague trip,

Of catapulting over the moon - a nightmare!

My Loneliness

Won't you visit

and see my loneliness?

Just one incomplete

poem on one white sheet.

Or just one incomplete

Black brushstroke on a 5 feet white canvas.

Or scrappy and incomplete

Note on my violin.

Won't you visit

To give me company?

Wearing Nothingness

Standing on the top of a hill at dusk

of my sad choices

Taking in all there was for two of us

Everything suddenly called me by name

Nothing seemed to me the same

The trees, the rocks, the flowers and the earth

Expressing their merry mirth

Joyous and happy and flowing

Every inch of their lives glowing

Where is the sadness I am so used to,

And the nagging pains that wreck me through

I searched for pain and sadness in the whole

Only to find it absent from their souls

They share my mind; not my tears

They share my joy; not my fears

Suddenly the peals of the mountain brook

Rocked the false foundation on which I stood

In a moment it vanished from view

Where did it vanish I don't have a cue

I was at once with the trees, the birds and the stars

With unbounded joy never mired

The universe welcoming me to its fold

With me basking in the glow of their gentle hold

Wonderful was it to be born again

Without the thoughts of greedy hateful gains

Wonderful was the warmth of the dress of nothingness

Without a trace of living weariness

I wear their hearts as they wear mine.

Woman Unchained

Stoking flames of love-soaked memories

Tales so puzzling but amazing

Appears as an overflowing cup of red wine

Mixed with blessed tears of pain filled brine

Heady, restless, moving

Must you ever stop loving?

Deep colourful stories hiding eternal truths

Facing buried imagination is uncouth

Daring to bare it all to let the light in

Seeing reality through play and fights

Free from the shackles of social oppressions

A woman unchained is full of chaotic expressions.

Imperfect Noble and Grand

The petals I worship you with are imperfect

With my mind and body, far less perfect

Traveled the great path of life with you

Secretly unknown and hidden from view.

Weary of travel to distant lands

Walking on the great path hand in hand.

Garments torn, dirty and bare

Bled by the thorns of Narmada without care

Where is a moment's unsullied loneliness

Reflecting perfect beauty and loveliness?

I gift you the passionate love of a man's heart

That feels and understands life from a worldly hearth.

With all your coyness of a woman of earth

Love spirals struggling up.

Imperfect; yet noble and grand

With arms outstretched, I stand – for You!

What a Great Day!

What a great day

Observing life at play

Emotions, feelings, likes, dislikes

Self-aggrandizement - lacking attention

ADD with distorted love and convoluted intelligence

At times stuck or springing to love

People wearing persona,

Masks, cloaks, flowing robes

Roaming in barren wilderness of the past

Searching endlessly

Waiting endlessly

Believing endlessly

Hoping endlessly

Fearing endlessly

Nothing easy; nothing certain

But life flows spontaneously - unpreturbed

Dissolving present like a misty curtain

Emerging for the future to behold

A fine sight to watch and hold

How meaningful are all that –

roaming, searching, waiting, believing, hoping, fearing?

Craving and clinging of darkened souls

Waiting to be liberated

Unaware of the gentle spirit

That comes gently knocking at the door

To be our guest to bliss and more.

A Sad Story

Today, I choose to write a sad poem

Of a beautiful lady

Searching and begged

Till she finds a man to love in depth

And the man in turn loved her too

Both saying sweet nothing – lies and assurances

Inflaming the passions of loving

Daring each other with uncommon bravado

Which normal mortals would think twice to do.

I don't know how to write this painful story

I can start, for instance,

'Under the starry sky with stars blue, silver and white.

"Or I can pen down, 'She loved him full which he returned at times."

This sounds so bland and uninteresting

Without the passion exciting

Let me try different something

On one night of an Indian spring

She held him near and kissed him so many times

And he whispered sweet nothings in her ears blushingly
inflamed

As how he can't but love the oozing love of her eyes,

Transforming into poems and paints

And not live without her

Loving her body and mind

Every inch of it.

That she collapsed under the infinite sky.

But he left her spirit at that without knowing why

Then on a fateful immense night in May

He bade farewell

By a long winding letter pregnant with feelings

Empty, harsh and without meanings

Igniting the dry uncared embers of love into blazing
fires.

She felt lost, outraged — castaway ensnared in a
deepening mire,

To understand this on that immense night made more
immense without him,

Her soul opened up to scatter flowing dew on grass

Enough to make dry Yamuna flood her banks again

How did it matter that his love couldn't keep her?

The night is still full of dewy stars without him with her

Far away someone sings

And her soul is lost without him

But keeps searching like the sweet sixteen

She is not sixteen any more with her tender confused face

But how does that all matter

Far, far away, someone sings the tune of conscience

To ask permission from all to continue their love at distance

She stands bare soulless without him

Her eyes still search for him

And her heart stops still with him

Bewildered she read his last response again

"I don't love you anymore but did love you too much

We were but no longer are the same anymore"

In the dead of the empty night

Her heart lets out the long wrenching primal cry

Of an animal wounded by Cupid's arrows of pain

Throbbing and heavy with no words in between

Seeking comforting thoughts from somewhere

Her voice was speechless searching the wind to touch her ears

Knowing that words wouldn't reach a heart so bleeding and sheared

She can't bear that he would desert her so

He belonged to her dreams of a dear happy married life so near

Ready to walk out of her present home

To carry his child in her

He belonged to her kisses as were her light voice, fair skin, soft eyes and her constant fears

She can't believe what she read, "I will no longer respond to you"

True that he no longer loved her but how long would that be?

Would oblivion be so cruel and long?

How long would that be into the cold nights starting now?

Because he held her attention on nights like this

With her soul lost in his

Now freed, untethered, roaming wildly in the skies

Would this be the last pain for her from him?

Would she sing again with the fullness of life she mimed?

Freed from the passionate fleshy craving love of ordinary mortals

Would she now be ethereal like Meera or Radha - immortal?

Emerging from the river of oblivion!

The Untold Story

As warm restless air of May pulsated impatiently

To meet the dusky cold sky of a young evening

We sat sipping strong brown coffee

Fluidly sensing precious moments creeping by

As silent heavy emotions easily bubbled up

We discovered more of the other with tales from many
burbs

Reaching the other with hesitant steps

Daring to bare untouched tassels of love secretly kept

Till a point came when everything tipped

Standing naked, suffused by understanding steeped

Savoring the delight of being crazy

In love with love and life, colorful and jazzy

Throwing cares to the winds

Creating beautiful minds

As her soft moist eyes expressed more, left untold

A story so passionately lingering to be put on hold.

I can't wait to write about it all tonight

I loved her and sometimes she loved me too, holding securely tight!

Longings of a Sunday Afternoon

As Sunday afternoon lengthens its shadows

Cool breeze chases down the meadows

Like kittens chasing their tails at play,

As I search for your oceanic eyes to allay,

My solitude blazes in inflamed waves

Reminding me of my escape from Plato's cave

Throwing my soul to the distant you -- warm

Like bees returning to hives in swarm

Afternoon merges to dusk

When old trees emanate a distinct old musk

As birds return to their nests twittering aloud

Till winking stars spring behind the sun-soaked clouds

As night gallops fast on its flowing black stallion

Creating silence in its wake, exposing buzzard's talons

Ripping my heart and body like wind battered kites

Shedding hopes of being allayed by your gently lapping

oceanic eyes.

Even if Cuckoo Sang more Sweetly

Imagine what my favourite park might be

If only a cuckoo sang more loudly

And forced other birds to sing the same

Or sealing them with steely ropes

My park would still be beautifully serene

Though uninviting to explore mysteries within

And all the powers that be

Wouldn't lead me up the gentle grassy path

Or rest under the shade of a tree strong and hard

To catch a glimpse of the delirious dusky bird

Even if the cuckoo sang more sweetly.

April Elephants

April lingers on with its itchy humidity

Huge black elephants float through the sky

Silently absorbing earthly vapors and secret desires

Bringing sudden downpours and chaotic Norwesters

That play in the minds of men.

Errant skies!

Relieving something or the other

Creating or destroying

Changing lives for good, bad or strange

As in a dream or with strumming of my son's guitar
strings

It is the mindset that matters

Hungry, guarded, open, dumb or selfless

The play goes on; expressions abound

As dark elephants trumpet merrily in the skies

Poetry of Life

I did patiently sit on the banks of dialogs and poetry
of life
Watching thoughts and emotions streaming by
Waiting to catch the brightest ones, though timid and
shy
Few did I catch and with them the seeds of Wisdom
did I sow
Melding them to make them grow,
This is all the Harvest I reaped
Came to water to fill voids within
And inhale sweet winds of changes wafting in
Feeling the faint cries of wisdom breaking free
Bleeding my heart for more.
Remembering striking up conversations with Dad
Immersed in the faint glow of yellowish light
Discussing all that bothered me at that instant
In my world and the environment that conversed

Remembering every bit of it

With the growing wisdom of a tree

Remembering my art teacher, Sanat Kar

Playfully pouring himself on my colorful shores

Adding a comment here or a few strokes there

Igniting me to think anew and share

Where a simple smile was enough to turn my head

Buzzing with creativity

Remembering my maths teacher Choudhury

Who drew me to love Venn, sets and binary

Never stating steps or thrusting himself on me

Gently letting me imagine what to do, not plan

Unfolding puzzles and riddles with playful shots

Or encourage cutting through Gordian knots

Remembering my design teacher A K Sen

Enveloped in silence with deep intent

Fluidly creating designs on blackboards

Attracting me to patterns not thoughts

Making me believe I could

Design an elephant when I wish to

Remembering my guru Tim Henry

Who answered when I asked keenly

Never defining, never definitive, never protecting

Always leaving enough room to reflect

Answering with 'May be, I think'

I remember all they shared

So openly free without guards

Never made me feel a student in awe

Never cajoling, never manipulating

No force, no punditry

Always in ever expanding dialogs

A flow never ever complete

Creating space to ask more and grow

Backed by courage to say 'I don't know'

In every case it was that of respect

Driven by love alloyed with curiosity unchecked

Leading into myriad unknown lands sprinkled with mines

Liberating me like the heady taste of sparkling wine

Now with dialogs over Facebook, Twitter and Linkedin

Still excited in the dusk of life with conversations

At times I miss that intoxicating taste of deadly wine

Of being face to face with reflections

Improving on mistakes and forgetting the past

Bouncing ideas to engage in serious play

Striking rich dialogs built with watery clay

Thirsty for those smiles, 'what ifs', questions, 'may be'
and storytelling

Unable to erase pleasures of trusting, loving, respecting
and playing

Still miss those life transforming stories the most

How do I keep waking myself up every morn?

To recreate the exciting childhood yet to pass

Behold

Keen to know what the future folds or unfolds

I looked at signs, stars, people and 101 ways to make it

come true

Seeking happiness and all the rewards that might bring

To create the future of my dreams

Keen to know what the future folds or unfolds

Looked for lucky signs that popped up serendipitously

Ran after them till I could run no more

But the future refused to fold or unfold for me

Keen to know what the future folds or unfolds

Looked at stars and my natal horoscope

Smugly content in destiny,

The future refused to fold or unfold for me

Keen to know what the future folds or unfolds

Believed people who could possibly do the trick

Followed them till I could follow no more

But future refused to fold or unfold for me

Keen to make the future fold or unfold

Wrote big plans to make it happen the way I wanted it to be

Worked hard till it couldn't be worked upon any more

But future refused to fold or unfold for me

Then as if by chance tired, broken, crestfallen

Gave up seeking the future anymore

No designing: no imagining: no doing

Then magically the present began to fold and unfold for me

Just when I heard the faintest of whisper deep below

Do I listen to this faintest whisper?

A clean intelligent whisper I haven't heard before

Pushing me somewhere I don't even know

An effortless silence whispering deep within

Dissolving rocks and filling craters

Folding and unfolding my present

Right in front of me.

Happy knowing that future holds nothing

And that it would never fold or unfold anything

It is as empty as empty can be

The present keeps folding and unfolding right in front

of me

As Shiva dances merrily

Forgetting You

I know you want me to forget your birthday

And stop wishing you.

I know you want me to forget the late night

We roamed the deserted streets of Udaipur

I know you want to forget the gifts we shared

And the numerous letters and photos in between

And the chats that wore long into sparkling nights.

Did you ever wonder why and how I would forget you?

You know what it feels like

To look out onto the streets from my window

To see teeming millions flow by but still spot you.

You know what it feels like

To gaze at the crystal moon and see you

And how everything carries me to you.

Even the leaves of the trees around the lake

Absorbed the energy of our feelings

Only to scatter all around in Autumn

Passing the message to every passer by

How do we deny?

Did you wonder how would I stop loving you?

Well that was clear in my mind.

If you stop loving me little by little

I would stop loving you little by little

If you stop loving me all of a sudden

I would forget you suddenly.

Because in love it is not two

You can't be half alive and half dead

It must be alive or dead -- nothing in between.

The moment you leave me stranded at your shores

Forbidding me to mingle with the waves and build sand castles

I shall at once take wings to fly off to seek another ocean

Who allows me to play on her shores with all my imagination

So long you think mad

That we are destined for each other

The fire burns bright

Nothing is dead or ever forgotten

Though I have deleted all your emails and Whatapp messages.

Have you deleted mine?

It was painful,

But I still love you,

Or do I still?

Be Good; Do Well

Remembering my first day at school

Mother saying "Be Good"; "Do Well"

As we walked up to the big school felt tension rise in the hand that held

Walking up the stairs to class

Never turned back to see her tense face

With "Be Good" and "Do Well" still buzzing in my head

After class, she rushed in lovingly embrace

"Were you good? Did you do well?"

Yes mom I did, I didn't speak.

Leave me alone Mom.

Why do you need to know I was good and did well.

A year passed, I showed Mom my rank card 10th out of 54

Was it good; Did I do well?

"Not really, could have done much better", Mom frowned

But I learned the difference between 'May I', 'Can I' and 'I will'

"That's not very useful, Dear" she said.

Year by year I became good to better

Choosing the path of perfection

Waiting to see a smile on my mother's face

Neglecting everything else I could do

Then I could do no better anymore

There was no more space left to do

I finally reached the dreaded spot

Where maturity takes over

Are you now happy Mom?

"Yes dear, but Be Good and Do Well"

At 54, my son rings me up to ask

"Dad, where have you reached now?"

Nowhere son, there is nothing more to do

The path of perfection I chose is dead

Quo vadis

I have changed my path

A path more fulfilling

A path more loving

A path more whole and new

"Why is that Dad", he asks

It is a path where I need not ask, 'May I?' 'Can I?'

Or ask, "Was I good?" and "Did I do well?"

I only need to say 'I will!"

A path free of perfection

Since the whole can never be good or bad

I needn't think of 'Be Good' and 'Do well'.

No pretensions; no tensions

Free to live life in gay abandon

Just what life was meant to be.

"What do you ask me to do, Dad"

Be whole to enjoy what you do.

Cravingly Unfulfilled

Walking in the park I see

People walking past with speed

Busy maintaining their slender and not so slender skeletons

With flesh covering it

What a splendid life I suppose

Flesh and skeletons crawling in and out of bed

Craving desires never filled.

Lands are filled

Pockets are filled

Politicians are filled

Cities are filled

Streets are filled

Buses are filled

Brains are filled

Love remains unfilled

Mind remains unfilled

What is it?

Pent Up Tears

I have left everything behind

But haven't left you

You still slip in me like a delicate resonating crystal

Trembling with uneasy wounded love

In love we found each other so thirsty

Drying up waters of any river however mighty

In love, we found each other so fiercely hungry

Biting into each other wounded and angry

But you did wait for me

With the sweetness of your love, not wasted

What might I give you back other than pent up tears.

We Would come Together To Be

I am not becoming without you becoming too

You shield the harsh summer heat

Like the shady bush with flowers smiling blue

You are the womb that sustains

You are the center of attention and action

You are the flow when time stops for me

When others see me glow

Your invisible aura creates the flow

When others hear what I speak or write

They don't hear you -- the silence in between

Without your becoming, coming, suddenly inspiring

I am struck breathless

Since You are the life in the air I breathe

You are flowing, changing

You will; I will; both becoming

We shall come together to be

How Do I Touch Thee?

I am awed by your complete presence

Filled with the smell of the melting moon

Crushed with dry jasmine; peppered with the tiredness
of June

What secrets do you hold?

Where do you hide them?

How do I touch thee with my senses?

Through my carnal desires on a primal night melting
& melding?

Or through love without words?

Covering you with invisible kisses from points to
infinity

How do I discover the inner dimensions of your Necker
Cube?

Alas, vision locked cube by cube

Unable to embrace the whole!

As I Sit With You

As I sit with you

I see restless young waves strike

The forlorn weary old stones

Bursting into effulgent brightness

Tiny bright diamond droplets

Self-organizing into garlands touched by brine

Fit for queens

Only to break again into thousand thirsty spumes

Returning to the eternal becoming nothingness

Falling silent again, sealing it.

Waiting to erupt and rise

Creating and destroying varied forms

Deluding me to feel continuity of creation and death

While everlasting silence of nothingness punctuates
the two

I Don't Know Why She Cries?

Tears well up in her eyes

Hearing a song that touches somewhere

Or seeing fresh young pupil leaves spring to life

Tears roll down her cheeks

Smelling a dark red rose growing free

Or touching a child who smiles and chuckles with glee

Tears flood her

Tasting a plate of biriyani at Zeesan after a year

Or feelings aroused by the touch of a pair of loving lips

I don't know why she cries

It springs from unfathomable depths

Or from a pristine place where human words don't reach.

Not One; Not Two

Sun & its light

Ocean & its waves

Singer & his song

Writer & his story

Artist & his art

Dancer & her dance

Poet & her poem

Engineer & his designs

Bearing & its lubrication

Gas flow & its duct wall

Motor & its bearings

Rotor & its bearings

Bus bar & its joints

Bus bar & its capacitance

Leader & his followers

Organization & its employees

Working & its learning

Production & its demand

Productivity & its inventory

Earnings & its expense

Problems & its constraints

Context & its context

Management & its effectiveness

Mentor & his mentees

Cow & its meadow

Mother & her child

Father & his family

Husband & his wife

Beautiful lady & her beautiful necklace

Lover & his love

How do we separate one from the other?

Whom do we love?

Not One; Not Two.

Roses on the Shelf

I don't know from where these roses came,

And where would they go.

I don't know whether they are alive & blooming,

Or preparing to die for a transition to another life.

Or do they live and continue to live

In a newspaper or in a green cloth or in my mind.

They tell so much,

Yet so much remains untold.

What remains untold,

Mysteriously but gently sways my mind.

They expand and contract at the same time,

Dancing to the rhythm of life.